Brisco

Life As A Therapy Dog

Written by Margot Bennett

with help from Brisco

FETCH PRESS PUBLISHING

Copyright © 2021 by Margot Bennett.

Story and photography by Margot Bennett
Photo modifications created using Photo Lab
Book design by Kelly Lenihan
Cover Design by Michael York

Brisco, Life As A Therapy Dog/Margot Bennett—1st ed.
Published 11/2021
LCCN 2020919326
Hardcover ISBN 978-1735799001
Softcover ISBN 978-1735799018
Ebook ISBN 978-1735799025

Produced in the United States of America

This book is dedicated to Brisco,
my therapy dog partner.

In addition, this story honors therapy dog
teams around the world who volunteer
their time to help those in need.

*First and foremost, therapy dogs
provide unconditional love.*

Proceeds from *Brisco, Life As A Therapy
Dog* are donated to agencies providing
therapy dog services and training

Hello! My name is Brisco and I am a yellow Labrador Retriever.

I am a therapy dog, which means I give love and support to those who need it. Think of me as the softest, most comfortable "security blanket" you ever had!

My human mom and I work as a team to help people in our community.

- ♥ I curl up with kids while they read.
- ♥ I fetch balls to bring kids joy and laughter.
- ♥ I roll on my back so people can rub my belly and relax.

Turn the page to start my story!

Chapter 1
Brisco Finds a Forever Home

It all started on a chilly fall day. My human family came to pick me up when I was only eight weeks old. I had been surrounded by puppies my whole life.

My new mom picked me up and wrapped me in a warm, soft blanket. She gently tucked me into the car and we drove home, together.

I arrived at my forever home as a tiny little thing. I could barely sit up straight.

I wonder what it will be like to be part of a family?

Can you name some things Brisco might learn in his new home?

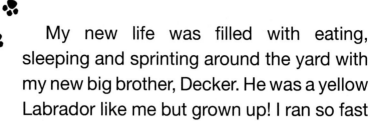

My new life was filled with eating, sleeping and sprinting around the yard with my new big brother, Decker. He was a yellow Labrador like me but grown up! I ran so fast playing, Mom called it my "Zoomies."

Decker and I spent quiet time together, too. One day, I shared my secret worry with him.

"*Woof*," I whispered to Decker. "*Will I be as loving and smart as you someday?*"

"*Yes*," Decker wisely said. "*I will teach you.*"

The first thing he taught me was to sit and wait for my food.

That was hard!

Every week he taught me more.

"*Eat slowly,*" Decker whispered as I gobbled my dinner.

"*No pulling,*" he insisted as we walked our humans.

"Me first," he quietly reminded me as we tucked ourselves in for the night. Then he crawled up onto our pillow.

I followed, resting my head on his.

"Woof," I whispered to him. *"Thank you for being my best friend."*

Chapter 2
Brisco Becomes a Big Brother

One day, a baby named Alex joined our family. At first I wasn't sure about his loud cries.

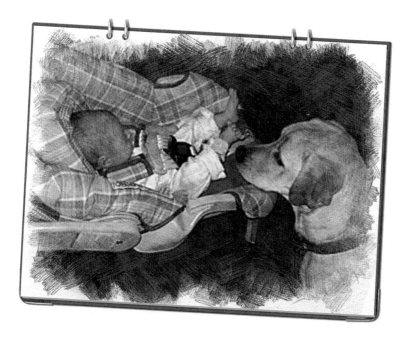

I wrinkled my nose when I sniffed him.
He smells brand new but he has no fur!

But I soon grew to love him, and we became best friends.

I missed Decker. He had been gone for almost a year. But I remembered all he taught me.

Now it was my turn to teach Alex things, just like Decker had taught me.

What do you think
Brisco will teach his
new family member?

"*Eat slowly,*" I suggested, as he stuffed food into his mouth.

"*Hold on tight,*" I nudged him as he held my leash.

"*Me first,*" I reminded him, as we crawled into bed for the night.

13

As Alex grew older, he started school. Every morning Mom and I walked him to the bus stop.

Every afternoon, I waited patiently, greeting him at the door when he got home.

I lay on my back, tail thumping, as he rubbed my belly. This was the best part of my day!

We hurried outside and I ran up into his fort, waiting for what was next.

Alex threw the ball and I raced after it. He giggled when I brought it back and dropped it at his feet.

Later, we spent quiet time together. Alex always planted a kiss on my head.

"*Woof*," I thought as I felt his love. "*You make me happy, my friend.*"

Mom watched our time together and knew there must be a way for me to share my big heart with others.

She signed me up for school to learn how!

At Alex's school, he learns to read and write.

I wonder what I will learn at MY school for dogs?

Chapter 3
Brisco Goes to School

My paws pranced as we arrived at our first class. What did I learn first?

Math?

Nope.

Reading?

Nope.

> **What fun things do YOU think Brisco will learn at his special school?**

First, I learned to avoid picking things up off the ground. For practice, I had to walk right past french fries!

"Mmm, they smell so good!" I thought as I inhaled their scent.

But I listened to my teachers and walked right past them. I also learned what to do when I heard these words: *"sit," "down," "stand," "bed," "stay"* and *"come."* I practiced walking on surfaces like grass, rubber mats, slippery floors and even bubble wrap! *POP! POP!*

You see, dogs don't wear shoes! My paws needed to get used to many surfaces.

I worked hard at learning, but at home, sometimes I was just silly. As I lay upside down on the soft bed in my kennel, I yawned.

I am so happy to be a dog!

For additional training, Mom took me to noisy places with lots of people.

I learned to ignore honking cars, strangers and other animals.

Children pointed at me and asked Mom, *"Can I pet your dog?"*

She always said *"Yes!"*

You see, petting THERAPY dogs helps people feel good. Therapy dogs are meant to be hugged and touched! This is different from SERVICE dogs, who are helping their human partners do tasks. Service dogs should NOT be distracted or interrupted.

Mom told me to "*sit*" and "*stay*" when someone came over to me.

It was hard for me.

I really wanted to get up and kiss them!

But I stayed in my "*sit*."

One day, a soft *woof* floated out of my mouth and grew into a loud bark. It surprised even me!

As part of my therapy dog training, I learned it is important NOT to bark, it might scare people we are trying to help.

Mom would give me a doggie treat to distract me when I barked at a squirrel or the vacuum or anything else. It was yummy learning to be calm and quiet!

I can speak but I must use my indoor voice.

At the end of every day I crawled into my bed, exhausted, and fell fast asleep.

Chapter 4
Brisco's Big Test

Soon my classes ended and it was time for my therapy dog test! This was an important step in becoming a therapy dog. Once I passed, Mom and I would be able to visit schools, hospitals and other places that might request a therapy dog team.

What do you think Brisco will have to do to pass his therapy dog test?

My stomach had butterflies when we arrived.

I am nervous!

Mom kneeled down to give me a hug and I instantly felt better. I had practiced hard.

I can do this!

My test began.

Mom told me *"down"* while she walked away and waited.

I stayed in a *"sit"* while some dogs walked around me. I did not bark or try to play with them.

This is easy!

The tester kneeled and petted me, touching my ears and my tail. That didn't bother me either.

Someone walked by me pushing a wheelchair. My eyes followed it, but I sat still and just watched it pass by.

We went outside, and I focused on Mom as we walked side by side. People with dogs passed by us, shuffling their feet. I stood in the parking lot as noisy toys rattled and raced by me.

I stayed calm the whole time!

Soon the test was over and everyone clapped for me. I received a special red heart to clip to my collar that said I was a therapy dog.

I did it!

I wanted to shout to the world!

I am officially a therapy dog now!

Chapter 5
Brisco As A Therapy Dog

It was time to get ready! Alex took a backpack to school. *What would I take when I went places?*

I lay on my bed in the kitchen, watching, as Mom put things into a bag decorated with pawprints.

I peeked inside the bag when she wasn't looking. *Shhhhh.* This is what I saw:

✓ tennis ball	✓ books	✓ towel
✓ bandana	✓ wipes	✓ ID card
✓ plastic bags	✓ stickers	✓ a mat

Wow! I need A LOT of stuff!"

How do you think Brisco might help people in his new role?

Mom glanced over at me just as Alex came over with a book. He lay down next to me and rested his head on mine. Mom smiled.

She knew kids reading to me would be perfect for my first job.

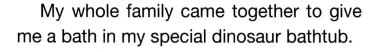

My whole family came together to give me a bath in my special dinosaur bathtub.

✓ Teeth cleaned? *Check!*

✓ Ears swabbed? *Check!*

✓ Fur brushed? *Check!*

I began to get nervous again.
Would other kids like reading with me as much as Alex does?

I walked into my first classroom. My heart raced. So many children were watching me! I lay quietly on my mat. The first little girl came over with a book and sat down next to me.

I could do this!

"Once upon a time..." she started reading, her hand trembling as she reached for my paw. I snuggled in tighter and thumped my tail.

Was I doing everything right? I snuck a peek at Mom.

"Woof?" I whispered to Mom.

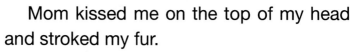

Mom kissed me on the top of my head and stroked my fur.

"*Good boy*," she told me.

I relaxed.

The little girl finished reading and squeezed me with a hug as she got up.

"*Woof*," I whispered to her. "*Thank you for reading to me!*"

Chapter 6
Brisco Helps The Shy Boys Talk

At home our phone began ringing every day. *"Brrrng!"* Many people called, asking for a therapy dog visit. I wagged my tail in excitement!

What will my future visits be like?

We soon went to see two young boys. They stood quietly on the other side of the room, shuffling their feet. Their mother told Mom the brothers did not talk very much and did not have many friends.

She hoped I could be a good friend to them.

Have you ever been shy? Or nervous? What do you think Brisco will do to help?

Friends share their toys. I will show them my favorite toy!

I trotted over and dropped my stuffed bear at their feet. They rubbed my fur but did not pick up my toy.

Maybe they want to play with something else?

I pulled out the tennis ball from my special bag. Mom asked the boys if they would like to throw the ball for me.

They both slowly nodded their heads. We went outside and Mom handed a ball to one of the boys. He threw it far into the grass. I ran after it and brought it back.

As I patiently waited for him to throw it again, I looked up and saw him smile!

The two boys took turns throwing the ball again and again. Soon, I began to hear their voices talking with Mom.

"*What was my favorite treat?*"

"*Where did I sleep?*"

They were asking questions about me!

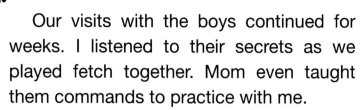

Our visits with the boys continued for weeks. I listened to their secrets as we played fetch together. Mom even taught them commands to practice with me.

Soon, it was time to move on to our next adventure.

"*Woof*," I whispered to them as we drove away. "*I'm so glad we became friends!*"

Now I got excited every time Mom grabbed my special bag, clipped on my red heart and tied a bandana around my neck. I knew we were going to visit someone I could help!

Chapter 7
Brisco's School Visits

We began visiting classrooms filled with children. Before they took turns reading to me, Mom showed the students how to approach and pet me. Sometimes there was a child who chose not to read or pet me. That was okay.

One girl needed help with her words.

"Woof," I whispered to her. *"Take your time, you are doing great!"*

Another boy was downright silly and read his book upside down. *Ha ha!*

"*Woof,*" I whispered to him. "*Thank you for making me laugh!*"

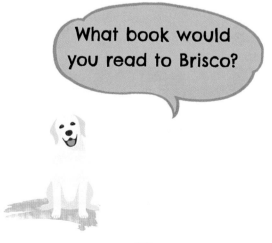

What book would
you read to Brisco?

One time, a little girl sat quietly next to me. After a while, I heard whispering sounds as she turned the pages, gently touching my paw as she read in a soft voice.

After a while she closed the book and returned to her seat. Tears streamed down the teacher's face, *"That little girl hasn't spoken a word since she started school."*

My tail wagged. I had helped her relax so she could speak her words out loud.

"Woof," I whispered across the room to her. *"Your voice is beautiful."*

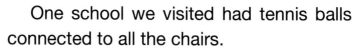

One school we visited had tennis balls connected to all the chairs.

Tennis balls? This is already my favorite place!

This visit was one big game of hide and seek. Mom told me to "*sit*" and "*stay*" and whispered "*no peeking!*" Each child took a turn hiding the tennis ball from my special bag, then they said excitedly, "*Okay Brisco, go find your ball!*"

Now, finding that ball was a challenge, but I always found it. Always! This type of visit was about giving the kids a fun break from their studies. I had a great time too!

I looked back at all the kids as we left. *You made this my best day ever!*

Chapter 8
Brisco's Family Fun

I loved being a therapy dog, but time with my family was important too.

What kinds of things do you think Brisco might like to do for fun?

Some days we visited the beach. Other times we took a trip to the mountains. Every so often, we all went for a really long hike at a nearby park.

I can smell a crab down there because my sense of smell is 100,000 times better than humans!

Wow! I can see a cow grazing in that field! My eyes may not see bright colors but I can view 240 degrees.

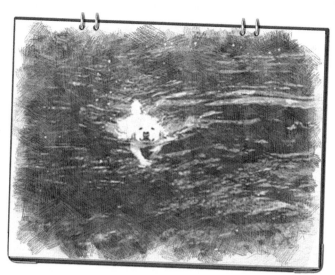

I even had a trip where I swam with the fish! My paws are made for paddling.

yum!

We gobbled up ice cream after every adventure. Always dog-friendly ice cream for me of course!

Every day we took walks and played games in the yard. When they ate lunch outside on summer days, I relaxed in the sun next to them.

In the winter, I enjoyed romping in the snow when everyone was home from school.

During holidays and special events, they even dressed me in fancy costumes!

I am the luckiest dog in the world!

I spent my therapy dog time visiting people I could help, AND I had a family at home I loved with all my heart. They took care of me, so I could help take care of others.

Chapter 9
Brisco Helps A Community

One day, Mom grabbed my special bag and drove us on a long car ride. When we arrived, it smelled salty and was VERY hot. My paw pads started sweating.

I was soon surrounded by people whose homes, cars and belongings had been damaged by a very strong storm called a hurricane. The people were tired and upset. They stroked my fur and fed me ice cubes. I seemed to bring them comfort.

"*Woof*," I whispered as we drove away. "*You will be okay.*"

As a therapy dog, I helped in many different ways!

Can you name some ways Brisco might be able to help out in YOUR community?

Here are a few of the other places I visited:

- ♥ **Colleges!** Mom and I visited older kids before their tests. This helped them to relax so they could study better.

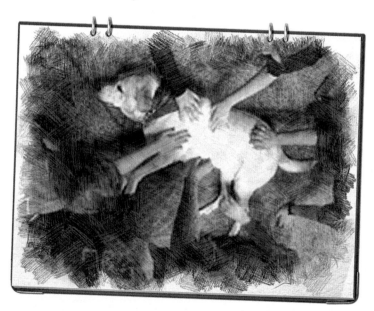

I loved the many hands that scratched my ears, rubbed my belly and glided over my fur.

♥ **Nursing Homes!** The older residents would share happy memories about their pets as I sat with them.

♥ **Education!** We talked to classes and large groups about the different ways therapy dogs help people.

There are so many different ways I have been able to help people!

Chapter 10
Brisco Becomes The Teacher

After nine years of being a therapy dog, my body grew tired.

Mom took me on fewer visits.

Every afternoon when Alex got home from school, he took me outside to tell me about his day. I thumped my tail with joy to show him I was listening.

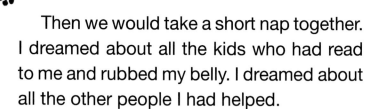

Then we would take a short nap together. I dreamed about all the kids who had read to me and rubbed my belly. I dreamed about all the other people I had helped.

Suddenly I was thirteen; where did the time go? Mom felt it was time for me to retire and rest.

"One more visit to listen to kids read," she said.

I wore my bandana for the last time.

Mom brought me into one of our classrooms. There were dozens of kids smiling, jumping up and down and clapping.

This was a surprise party for me!

All the kids came over to pet me, rub my belly, and thank me.

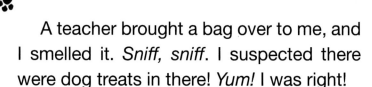

A teacher brought a bag over to me, and I smelled it. *Sniff, sniff.* I suspected there were dog treats in there! *Yum!* I was right!

Look at all the other things that were in the bag!

Mom read the cards to me that thanked me for my time and unconditional love. She had happy tears in her eyes. My therapy dog life had made a positive difference to so many people!

"*Woof,*" I sighed. "*Being ME has been amazing!*"

One day, my family brought home a puppy named Ely. He looked exactly like me, but little!

Hmmmm.

Mom had a new mission with Ely. He was going to be a Service Dog.

This time *I* would be the big brother!

Brisco has served people in so many ways: playing, listening and encouraging.

How might he help in his next role as teacher?

I will share my dog life with Ely, my toys, my walks, my bed and my family.

And teach him, like Decker taught me.

The first thing I taught him was to sit and wait for his food.

Ely will tell you, in his own words, about his journey. *Ely, Life As A Service Dog Puppy* is the next book in the series *Tails of Dogs Who Help!*

I am excited to see where this journey will lead my new friend!

Ely looks forward to seeing you soon!

As a service Dog, Ely will have a human partner. Can you think of some things Ely might be able to help his partner with?

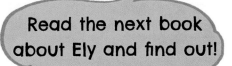

Read the next book about Ely and find out!

"Woof, the end!"

Did I catch your attention?

Let me tell you a few things about what therapy dogs can help with.

PHYSICAL HEALTH

reduce pain
lower blood pressure
improve heart health
be calming

READING SKILLS

lift spirits
provide comfort
decrease anxiety
encourage communication
reduce loneliness

MENTAL HEALTH

help kids focus
increase self-confidence
provide non-judgemental space
encourage the LOVE to read
improve literacy skills

Amazing, right?

Thank you for adding
Brisco, Life As A Therapy Dog to your
library. If your child enjoyed this story,
please consider posting a thoughtful
review on your child's behalf on Amazon
or other favorite book site. Your kindness
will make a difference for others
considering this book.

Proceeds from *Brisco, Life As A Therapy Dog* are donated
to agencies providing therapy dog services and training.

Acknowledgements

Brisco is registered with Alliance of Therapy Dogs
therapydogs.com

Alliance of Therapy Dogs (ATD) is an international registry of certified therapy dog teams. ATD provides testing, certification, registration, support, and insurance for members who volunteer with their dogs in animal-assisted activities. Their objective is to form a network of caring individuals and their special dogs that are willing to share smiles and joy with people, young and old alike.

For additional information on therapy dog organizations, visit:
petpartners.org • loveonaleash.org

To request visits from a local therapy dog team, please contact any of the above organizations.

Meet the Author

Margot Bennett has trained with over 10 dogs during the last 25 years, serving as a puppy raiser for nine service dogs as well as partnering with Brisco for therapy dog work. She firmly believes all dogs have a purpose and that belief has propelled her to volunteer in multiple dog placement programs that service communities.

Brisco, Life As A Therapy Dog, is her first children's story, using photos throughout Brisco's life to illustrate his journey into therapy dog work. Brisco's story is the first in her book series *Tails Of Dogs Who Help*. In telling the stories of the dogs she has raised, she is excited to teach the message of what our dogs can do for us, whether it be through therapy or through service.

The author's hope is these books will be a fun way to educate kids about how these dogs become who they are meant to be by telling it through the eyes of the dog.

Margot lives in North Carolina with her husband and four children. When she's not working with dogs, helping with homework or volunteering at schools, you can find her hiking, swimming or hiding out in her nook working on scrapbooking, playing the drums and thinking of more ways to outreach with future dogs.

She is excited to be working on her next book in the series. *Ely, Life as a Service Dog Puppy* will be available soon.

Want to learn more?

Visit Margot's website

dogswhohelp.com

Follow all the Bennett dogs on Instagram!

@tailsofdogswhohelp · #tailsofdogswhohelp

and on Facebook

facebook.com/Tails-Of-Dogs-Who-Help

Made in the USA
Columbia, SC
26 November 2021